The Bear Man

Keith Scott

Illustrations by Steve Hill

hancock house

ISBN 978-0-88839-655-6

Cataloging in Publication Data

Scott, Keith, 1936–
    The bear man / Keith Scott ; illustrations by Steve Hill.

    ISBN 978-0-88839-655-6

    1. Bears—Behavior—Juvenile literature. 2. Bear
attacks—Prevention—Juvenile literature. I. Hill, Steve,
1966– II. Title.

QL737.C27S355 2008   j599.78'15   C2008-902182-7

Printed in Indonesia — TK PRINTING

*We acknowledge the financial support of the Government of Canada through the
Book Publishing Industry Development Program (BPIDP) for our publishing activities.*

Editor: Ingrid Luters
Production : Ingrid Luters

Illustrations by Steve Hill, musician and artist

I would like to thank Steve Hill for understanding
my unusual occupations and illustrating them
with so much talent and humor. — KEITH SCOTT

Published simultaneously in Canada and the United States by

HANCOCK HOUSE PUBLISHERS LTD.
19313 Zero Avenue, Surrey, B.C. Canada V3S 9R9
(604) 538-1114 Fax (604) 538-2262
HANCOCK HOUSE PUBLISHERS
1431 Harrison Avenue, Blaine, WA U.S.A 98230-5005
(604) 538-1114 Fax (604) 538-2262

Website: **www.hancockhouse.com**
Email: **sales@hancockhouse.com**

My name is Keith "The Bear Man" Scott.

I was born in Saint John, New Brunswick, Canada on April 17, 1936.

When I was a boy, I lived across the street from Victoria School. The school had a basketball court and I played every day — with friends, by myself, in the summer, and even in the winter.

You don't need much equipment to have fun playing basketball.

I started with a pair of runners that I bought at a Salvation Army thrift store for 50 cents and a basketball that I found abandoned in the schoolyard.

I invented new trick shots like sliding on the ice half way down the court while trying to get the shot away before ending up in the snowbank.

When I wasn't playing basketball in the schoolyard, I spent my spare time hiking in the woods looking for wild animals.

I played basketball in high school and ended my graduating year winning the league's scoring title and was named player of the year and member of the all-star team.

Some kids I went to school with called me a sissy when I wouldn't smoke with them. One boy said to me, "You're not a man if you don't smoke."

My mother said to me, "If you were meant to smoke, there would be a pipe sticking out of your head."

A teacher told me, "Never drink, never smoke, and never take drugs. If you never do these things, you will be able to play basketball all your life."

I listened to both of them.

After high school I played professional basketball for a team called the House of David. They were advertised as the world's best basketball team. I had to grow a beard to be on the team. I was the ballhandler and had to do all the tricks. One part of the show consisted of me dribbling the ball while lying on the floor.

I also played for a team called the Harlem Aces. I was the only white player on an all-black team.

During my basketball career I played against many great players, including Bob Cousy of the Boston Celtics and Wilt Chamberlain when he played for the Harlem Globetrotters. Wilt Chamberlain was 7'1" tall — the tallest player I ever played with or against.

Because I was always the only non-drinker on the team, I was the one who would usually drive to the next game.

I drove the side roads to the next game hoping to see wildlife. My team-mates weren't too enthusiastic about wildlife though — especially when they came too close.

By 1976 I was no longer playing professional basketball. I spent my time hiking and looking for bears. I started taking lots of photographs and began to learn about bear behavior.

The first thing I learned was that surprising a bear at close range is very dangerous.

Sometimes when I was out hiking I got into some awkward situations. I learned how to escape dangerous encounters with bears; but more importantly, I learned how to prevent them.

Bears have a keener sense of smell than humans and are attracted to the food smells of camping.

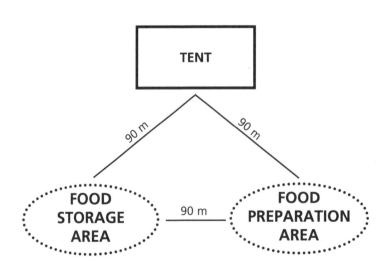

Cook your food 90 meters (300 feet) away from your tent and store your food 90 meters (300 feet) from your tent and food preparation area. This is called the triangle method of camping.

Even the smell of hot chocolate can attract a bear. Bears can also smell blood, so any fish you catch should be cleaned away from your tent.

Other small animals are attracted by food odors as well. Many small animals in one location will in turn attract bears.

Bears are nocturnal, which means they are more active just before dark, during the night and early in the morning.

Black Bears

General size:

In most cases black bears are smaller than grizzly bears. They can grow to a length of 1.8 m (6 feet) and can weigh up to 170 kg (375 pounds) They have a smaller shoulder hump than grizzly bears and their snout is longer.

Color:

Black bears are usually charcoal black with some having a patch of white fur on their chest. But black bears can also be light or dark brown in color and rare ones can be yellowish white, pure white or bluish black.

Claws:

Their claws can be over 5 cm (2 inches) long. They are smaller and more tightly curved than grizzly claws, which make them good for climbing trees. Their claws are sharp in the spring when they come out of hibernation but become more blunt by autumn after a season of digging and climbing trees.

FRONT CLAWS

Grizzly Bears

General size:

Compared to black bears, grizzlies are larger. The can grow to a standing height of over 3 m (10 feet) and can weigh over 450 kg (1,000 pounds). They have a very prominent hump on their shoulder. Their face is dished (flat) which gives their head a more concave profile.

Color:

Their fur can be black or brown and the tips of their hairs can be silver colored.

Claws:

The front claws of an adult grizzly can be 10 cm (4 inches) long. Because their claws are so long and only slightly curved they cannot climb trees as well as black bears, but they will if they feel threatened. Their hind tracks look very much like human barefoot tracks because their hind claws are shorter than their front claws and seldom show up in their tracks. Just like black bears, their claws are sharp in the spring and become more blunt from digging and scratching.

FRONT CLAWS

Don't block the path of a bear walking in your direction. Give bears the right-of-way. When a bear is on a hiking trail coming towards you, get off the trail.

Bears are very sensitive to human body language. When you are close to a bear, don't make quick movements.

Don't crowd a bear or group of bears.

Some dogs are good bear dogs, but many dogs will chase bears and in return the bears will chase the dog right back to you.

Dogs running loose in the woods may cause a tragic bear–dog–human incident.

If you see a bear cub, don't approach it. A cry or any sound from the cub will bring the sow to her side within seconds.

One time, when I was hiking, a cub came out of the bushes and sniffed my boots. I knew the sow was only a short distance from the cub because I could see twigs moving behind it.

Knowing that bears get excited when anything makes quick movements, I backed up slowly while facing the bear. At a safe distance away, I turned and hiked out of the area.

When hiking with a group that includes children, always have one adult at the front and one adult at the back of the group.

If you find fresh bear tracks, sing or talk loudly. Let bears that might be nearby know where you are. Bears want to avoid you just as much as you want to avoid them.

Never approach a bear feeding on garbage, apples, grasses, etc. The bear will become aggressive and protect his food.

Facing the bear, back up slowly and give the bear more room. Don't run when you are close to a bear. In most cases, bears will try to catch anything running away from them.

Black bears are very good tree climbers. Grizzly bears can climb trees too but seldom do. Just don't assume they won't.

When charged by grizzly bears, I have laid down and sometimes rolled up into a ball to protect my vital parts. Twice I have had bears sniff my body and then move on.

Since bear spray was invented I have it with me all the time. I've had to use it four times. All four times I've sprayed a bear they ran in the opposite direction. The effects of the bear spray last up to one hour. After that the bear is back to normal.

When I go hiking into the back country, I usually take too much with me, but I always bring everything back, including my garbage. When I get home I recycle everything I can.

I never cut a tree down for firewood. I cut up dead wood. And I always make sure my fire is out and cold before leaving my campsite.

"Goodbye, Keith. See you next year."

Keith Scott "The Bear Man"

Since 1975, Keith Scott has made his living delivering lectures and slide presentations on the subjects of bears and bear safety, appearing at over 100 schools a year.

A popular part of Keith's presentation is his basketball demonstration, which illustrates the lesson he took to heart years ago when he was a young boy: "If you don't drink, or smoke, or do any drugs, you can play basketball for the rest of your life." And he does.

If you would like Keith Scott to visit your school, you can contact him at:

Keith Scott
66 Sunset Dr.
Fredericton, NB
E3A 1A1
1-505-472-1825

Other bear books by Keith Scott published by HANCOCK HOUSE PUBLISHERS

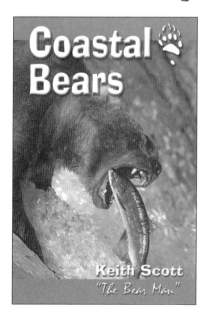

Coastal Bears
ISBN-10: 0-88839-626-0
ISBN-13: 978-0-88839-626-6
5.5" x 8.5", sc, 80 pages

The Great Bears of Hyder, AK & Stewart, BC
ISBN-10: 0-88839-496-9
ISBN-13: 978-0-88839-496-5
5.5" x 8.5", sc, 80 pages

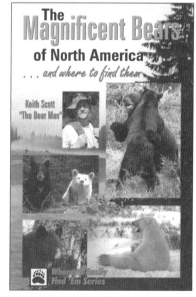

The Magnificent Bears of North America
ISBN-10: 0-88839-494-2
ISBN-13: 978-0-88839-494-1
5.5" x 8.5", sc, 160 pages

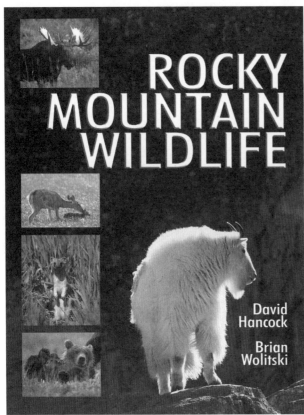